D1120040

Tell Your Parents

All About Electric and
HYBRID
CARS
and Who's Driving Them

STEPHANIE BEARCE

Mitchell Lane
PUBLISHERS

P.O. Box 196
Hockessin, Delaware 19707
Visit us on the web: www.mitchelllane.com
Comments? email us: mitchelllane@mitchelllane.com

PUBLISHERS

Tell Your Parents

All About Electric and Hybrid Cars
Green Changes You Can Make Around Your Home
How to Harness Solar Power for Your Home
How to Use Wind Power to Light and Heat Your Home
How You Can Use Waste Energy to Heat
and Light Your Home

Copyright © 2010 by Mitchell Lane Publishers

PUBLISHER'S NOTE: The facts on which the story
in this book is based have been thoroughly
researched. Documentation of such research
can be found on page 43. While every possible
effort has been made to ensure accuracy, the
publisher will not assume liability for damages
caused by inaccuracies in the data, and
makes no warranty on the accuracy of the
information contained herein.

PLB / PLB2

Special thanks to automotive consultant Ed
Scarfe for his help on this book.

Printing   2   3   4   5   6   7   8   9

**Library of Congress
Cataloging-in-Publication Data**
Bearce, Stephanie.
   All about electric and hybrid cars / by
Stephanie Bearce.
      p. cm.
   Includes bibliographical references and index.
   ISBN 978-1-58415-763-2 (library bound)
   1. Electric automobiles—Juvenile literature. 2.
Hybrid electric cars—Juvenile literature. I. Title.
TL220.B42 2010
629.22'93—dc22

                                      2009004528

CONTENTS

Words in bold type can be found in the glossary.

Toyota Prius

STARS AND CARS

It's a fancy Hollywood party, and all the famous movie stars are invited. You might expect to see them driving up in big limousines, expensive sports cars, and shiny new SUVs. But actress Cameron Diaz buzzes up in her new **hybrid** car. It's not big. It's not fancy. It's not even expensive. Instead, it is a car that can help the environment.

Diaz is one of many famous people who are concerned about pollution and trying to make the planet Earth a healthier place to live. She could afford to buy any car she wants, but she drives a small gasoline-electric hybrid car because it gives off very little air **pollution**.

A hybrid car is a car that can run on two or more fuel sources. Most modern hybrid cars are powered by both an electric motor and a gasoline engine. A traditional car has

Cameron Diaz

Tesla Roadster

only a gasoline or diesel engine. These engines are good for traveling long distances, but they cause pollution. They make the air unhealthy for plants and animals. Electric motors do not emit exhaust, but most of them can travel only short distances—between 40 and 120 miles—before they must have their batteries recharged. A hybrid car uses both an engine and a motor to make the car run. The engine not only powers the car, but it also recharges the batteries as it runs. Hybrid cars put out far less pollution than traditional cars, yet they can still travel several hundred miles before refueling.

Cameron Diaz drives her hybrid car all over the Los Angeles area. In 2002, she bragged about her car on the *Tonight Show with Jay Leno*. She explained that her hybrid

Cameron Diaz speaks about the environment at the Live Earth Concert in New Jersey's Giant Stadium, 2007.

car keeps the air clean with its electric motor, and it saves gasoline.

Diaz is a member of the Environmental Media Association, and she often speaks to groups about how to reduce pollution. She says that if everyone would just make one **green** change in his or her life, they would see amazing differences in the world. Driving a hybrid car is one way a person can reduce his or her **carbon footprint**.

Living green means living in a way that respects natural resources and that protects people and other things living on the planet, now and in the future. A carbon footprint is the amount of carbons or pollution that a person generates in everyday activities, such as driving a car or mowing the lawn, or even using electricity in the house. Carbon dioxide is one type of pollution that is given off by gasoline-powered cars. Driving an electric or hybrid car puts less carbon into the air than driving a traditional car. It helps reduce a person's carbon footprint.

Former Vice President Al Gore is another famous person who drives a hybrid car. Gore also believes that driving a hybrid car can help reduce pollution. He made a movie about the problem of pollution and how it is causing **global warming**. This movie, called *An Inconvenient Truth*, explains how pollution from cars is making the earth too hot for many types of plants and animals to live.

Traditional cars are responsible for most of the air pollution on the planet. It is estimated that cars and trucks

Al Gore

CARBON DIOXIDE EMISSIONS

POLLUTION FROM A STANDARD CAR

POLLUTION FROM A STANDARD SUV

According to the Environmental Defense Fund, cars in the United States give off over 33 million tons of carbon dioxide every year. That is one-fifth of all the carbon dioxide in the whole world. Driving a big truck or sport utility vehicle (SUV) creates even more pollution. A large gasoline-engine truck or SUV gives off 43 percent more pollution than a midsize car.

that run on **petroleum** products give off more air pollution than all the power plants in the world.

Ozone is another chemical that destroys the earth's atmosphere. Motor vehicles make 72 percent of all ozone. They make 52 percent of all **smog**. With this much pollution made by cars, you can see why Gore thinks we should change the types of vehicles we drive.

He also believes that as more people learn the truth about pollution, they will want to get involved. People will want to make the changes necessary to help save the planet. Besides driving hybrid cars, Gore recommends using energy-efficient appliances and planting trees. Recycling plastic bottles and newspapers is another way to help keep the earth clean.

Actor Brad Pitt agrees with Gore and Diaz. He traded in all of his gasoline cars and now drives only hybrid cars. Pitt wants to use his fame to help the planet. He has spoken out about air pollution and oil **conservation** to many groups. He is a member of Global Green USA, and is working to help build homes with environmentally friendly products. He even narrated several episodes of *e2: The Economies of Being Environmentally Conscious*, a television series about how to be responsible for the environment. Pitt looks forward to the day when every American driver can own a car that does not rely on **fossil fuels**.

Brad Pitt arrives in style in his environmentally friendly hydrogren-electric hybrid car. When he's not making movies, he uses his celebrity status to promote green living.

In 2009, most hybrid cars were using gasoline and electricity. However, scientists and car manufacturers had begun experimenting with other types of hybrid cars. Pitt drives a **hydrogen-** and electric-powered car. This car doesn't use any gasoline. It uses hydrogen to run an engine. Because hydrogen is one of the chemicals in clean air, a hydrogen hybrid car gives off very little pollution. The main product it puts into the environment is water.

So why doesn't everybody drive hydrogen cars? In 2009, the technology was still very expensive. Only wealthy people could afford them. Pitt hopes that if he can get other famous people to buy the cars, it will make the cars popular. For

BMW exhibited this hydrogen car in 2007. While BMW and other car companies may be ready to roll a lot of these cars off their production lines, drivers need access to filling stations.

The first station in North America to sell both hydrogen and gasoline is in Washington, D.C. It was set up as a joint project between Shell Hydrogen and General Motors Corporation.

example, if a lot of people want to buy hydrogen cars, more of them will be made, and the price may go down.

Hydrogen is also hard for the average person to get. Unlike the vast number of gas stations, there are very few hydrogen filling stations. But that will change if more people buy the hydrogen cars. In the future, stations may be very different. Instead of gas pumps, there may be electric batteries for some cars and hydrogen fuel cells for other cars.

That's the future Cameron Diaz, Al Gore, and Brad Pitt are hoping for. They want to see clean cars that do not use a **nonrenewable** resource such as gasoline. And they really want to see cars that make Earth a cleaner, greener place to live.

DRIVEN TO POLLUTION

How often do you ride in a car? Every day? More than once a day? Most Americans spend a lot of time in the car. They use cars to go to work, to school, and to the store. They ride in cars to visit relatives and to go on vacation. Cars are the primary source of transportation in the United States. According to the U.S. Department of Transportation, in 2008 there were over 250 million passenger cars in the United States—one for nearly every person in the country.

Driving a car has a lot of advantages. You can go exactly where you want and when you want. You don't have to wait for a bus to pick you up. You don't have to walk a long way to a train station. And you can easily drive from one state to another. Americans like cars because they are convenient.

The trouble is that making all those cars work causes a lot of pollution. And it's not just while they're on the road. Gasoline is used to make the engine run. The gasoline is made from petroleum oil found in the earth. This oil has to be drilled and taken from the ground. The drills give off pollution as they work. Then the oil has to be **refined**— separated into its usable parts. The gasoline is then transported to filling stations in huge tanker trucks that also cause pollution. Finally, an engine causes pollution as it burns the gasoline.

During the refining process, petroleum oil is separated. The heaviest oil settles to the bottom of the tank. The lightest oil floats on the top. Gasoline is made from the lightest oils. Kerosene and diesel oil are medium weight, and

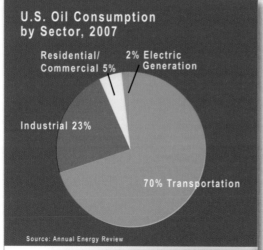

U.S. Oil Consumption by Sector, 2007

Residential/Commercial 5%

2% Electric Generation

Industrial 23%

70% Transportation

Source: Annual Energy Review

Transportation is the largest user of petroleum in the U.S. Trucks, cars, and airplanes use more oil than all other areas combined.

the heaviest oil is used to make things like asphalt and plastic. After the oils are separated, they are heated to high temperatures to burn off any unwanted chemicals. Every step of this process creates more pollution.

The oil refineries emit chemicals that go into the air and water. The refineries have to follow special guidelines set up by the U.S. government, but even with the guidelines, there is still pollution. The rules allow each refinery to emit 25 tons of pollution every year. It is estimated that worldwide, refineries give off 350,000 tons of pollution a year.

The Energy Information Association reported that in 2006, Americans were using 385 million gallons of gasoline every day. There were 299 million people living in the United States. On average, every man, woman, and child in the U.S. was using more than a gallon of gasoline every day. Another way to look at it: In 2007, Americans burned 142 *billion* gallons of gasoline—some 16 million gallons per *hour.*

The United States can't make enough gasoline for all its needs. There are not enough refineries in the country to make the amount of gasoline that Americans use. And America uses more gasoline than what can currently be pumped out of U.S. oil wells. Only about 34 percent of all gasoline is produced from U.S. oil. Americans have to buy the rest of their oil from foreign countries.

Not only is it hard to obtain, but oil is a nonrenewable resource. There is only so much oil in the earth. When it is all used up, there won't be any more. Since it takes millions of years for oil to form, it is important to use what we have wisely.

Pollution from cars and other petroleum-burning machines may cause lung cancer, respiratory problems, urban smog, and acid rain, which can damage buildings and plant life. It may also cause global warming—an increase in the temperature of the earth. Global warming could destroy the earth's food webs. It can also cause polar ice caps to melt. This makes the ocean levels higher, which will cause flooding around the world. Animals that depend on the polar ice, such as polar bears, will also suffer. These are some of the many problems caused when people burn gasoline.

To reduce these problems, many people want to change the types of vehicles we drive. If we use less gasoline, it will keep the planet cleaner. If we change the way we use cars, we can help save the plants, the animals, and even people.

One way to use less gasoline is to drive a hybrid car. A gasoline-electric hybrid car uses an electric motor part of the time and a gasoline engine part of the time. When the electric motor is running, the car does not release toxic chemicals in the air. This is one way to cut down the amount of air pollution.

Many people who are concerned about the planet already own and drive hybrid cars. The Toyota car company announced that between 2001 and 2008, they had sold one million Prius hybrid cars in the United States.

This is good news for the environment—but there is even more good news coming. Scientists and inventors are working on other types of hybrid vehicles. One is a hydrogen car that uses hydrogen fuel cells and an electric motor to power the car. This vehicle is extremely green, but the technology is new and very expensive. It can cost $100,000 for a car like this. Scientists hope to find ways to make the cars less expensive.

Plug-in hybrid cars are another option for drivers. This type of hybrid uses extra batteries. It has a plug that connects to an outlet in your garage. The car can be recharged while you are at home. This kind of hybrid makes almost no pollution.

Another kind of hybrid vehicle is a **bio-diesel** hydrogen hybrid. This car uses bio-diesel as the primary fuel and hydrogen as a secondary source. Bio-diesel is made from plant oils like soybean oil. The cars can even use oil that is recycled from a restaurant's fryer. Bio-diesel hydrogen hybrids burn this oil and use hydrogen fuel cells. For long distances, the engine uses the recycled vegetable oil. For shorter trips, it is powered by the hydrogen fuel cells. This car does not have to use any gasoline. The vegetable oil burns cleaner

Bio-diesel fuel, made from plants, is a renewable resource. Biofuels are sustainable alternatives to petroleum products.

Many people think hybrid cars are the same as electric cars. This is not true. An all-electric car must be plugged in when the battery gets low. A hybrid car uses an electric motor, rechargeable batteries, and an engine that burns fuel. The engine starts when the battery gets low, and it charges the battery. There are plug-in hybrid cars, but not all hybrid cars need to be plugged into an electrical outlet to recharge.

Nissan electric car, the Pivo 2; its cabin swivels over the wheels.

than gasoline, so it makes less pollution. And even better, when the oil has been recycled from a restaurant fryer, the fumes from the car smell like french fries.

As scientists experiment, they will find ways to make the new cars less expensive. They may also find ways to make smaller, more powerful batteries. Or they may discover another type of fuel for engines. It will take some time for all of the new cars to be built, but in the future, it may be possible for every driver to have an electric or hybrid car.

Mixte

HYBRID HISTORY

Hybrid cars are not new. The first cars invented were often powered by more than one form of energy. The first hybrid car was built in 1899 by the Lohner-Porsche company. Called the petro-electric Mixte, it used a gasoline engine and electric motors in the hubs of the front wheels. It was exhibited at the 1900 World's Fair in Paris and was quite a sensation. The car manufacturing company is now known simply as Porsche.

Automobiles did not start off using gasoline as a fuel source. The first vehicle that did not need horses to pull it was powered by a steam engine. It was invented by Nicolas Cugnot in 1769. The car looked more like a modern tractor, and it used a huge steam boiler to make it run.

Rudolf
Diesel

Right:
Karl Benz

Many of the first cars ran with steam-powered engines, but oil or gasoline was burned to heat water in a boiler. The steam from the boiling water then powered the engine. While they did use some gasoline, these cars were mainly powered by the pressure in the steam.

In 1893, German inventor Rudolf Diesel invented an engine that is now called a diesel engine. He said his engine could run on vegetable oils and peanut oils. He displayed his engine at the World's Fair in 1911. But he died two years later, and other manufacturers built his engine to run on a petroleum product—diesel fuel.

It was around 1886 that the first practical gasoline-powered vehicles were invented. Working separately, both Gottlieb

In 1919, electric cars could be charged through any electric outlet. The cord from this car's battery runs to an outlet inside the barn.

Daimler and Karl Benz made cars that used a gasoline engine. But gasoline-powered cars were not popular with the public. They were noisy, and people hated the smell of the gasoline fumes. They also needed a hand crank to start them. Sometimes the engine would "kick back." If that happened while the person was still holding the crank, the person's arm could break.

The first electric cars were built in the 1830s. In 1899 and 1900, electric cars outsold all other types of cars. The electric cars had a lot of advantages. They did not vibrate or smell bad like gasoline cars. They did not need a hand crank. And they did not need to shift gears. Other cars in the early 1900s had manual gear shifts. Because the electric car did not have to shift gears as the speed changed, it was much easier to learn how to drive.

In the early 1900s, electric and hybrid cars were advertised across the U.S.

Changes in gasoline cars leveled the playing field with electric cars. In 1897, Hiram Percy Maxim invented the **muffler**. It made gasoline cars much quieter. Then in 1912, Charles Kettering invented the electric starter. People no longer had to crank the engine to start it.

In the early 1900s, there were not many paved roads. Most good roads were in cities. To travel farther, people took trains or still used horse-drawn wagons. An electric car did not need to go long distances because there were no roads good enough for any type of car.

As cars grew more popular, communities across the country started building smoother roads. Drivers wanted to use their cars to go from one town to another. They wanted to take longer trips in their cars. The electric car just couldn't travel as far as a gasoline car.

By the 1960s, cars clogged the streets of cities and turned blue skies to smog gray.

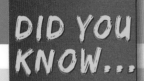

DID YOU KNOW...

Cars are the most recycled consumer product in the United States. The United States Council for Automotive Research reports that 15 million vehicles are recycled every year. On average, 84 percent of a vehicle can be recycled.

The big problem with the electric car was the weight of the batteries. Gasoline weighed much less than the heavy batteries used to power the electric car. Because they were lighter, gasoline cars could travel much faster—and they could travel longer distances. And 100 years ago, gasoline was very cheap. Most people decided they wanted to drive gasoline cars. By the 1930s, almost all cars on the road were gasoline powered.

In the late 1960s, scientists began to realize just how much pollution was coming from gasoline-powered cars. People who lived in large cities with a lot of cars started to notice that the air was not clear. In places like Los Angeles, the sky was often hazy and brown with smog. Scientists who sampled the air found that it was full of pollution, mostly from cars.

A book titled *Silent Spring* by Rachel Carson was published in 1962. It was the first serious look at how pollution harms the earth. People then started to worry about how cars were affecting the environment. The government made new laws that required cleaner-burning gasoline. But there was still pollution. There were just too many people driving too many cars.

California Governor Arnold Schwarzenegger admires a Saturn hybrid engine at the Los Angeles Auto Show. California has been a clean-car leader for decades.

Today, inventors, scientists, car makers, and the government are all working on ways to stop the pollution. Building hybrid cars seems to be a step in the right direction.

The two-door Honda Insight was the first modern electric-gasoline hybrid introduced to the United States. Released in 1999, it could travel an estimated 61 miles per gallon (mpg) in the city and 70 mpg on the highway. The Insight was quickly followed by the Toyota Prius in 2000. The four-door Prius has been popular with people across the United Sates. When other car manufacturers saw how popular the Prius was, they also began making hybrid cars.

Hybrid vehicles are not just tiny two-seat cars. There are vans and SUVs—and even pick-up trucks—that use a hybrid engine-motor system. By 2009, you could buy just about any type of car you wanted with a hybrid motor.

Hydrogen-electric hybrid cars are also available. Honda has been selling a hydrogen fuel cell car called the FCX Clarity that can be purchased in California. BMW, Mercedes, and Toyota all offer hydrogen fuel cell cars for sale. Most of them are sold in Europe.

In 2006, Tesla Motors in California began producing the Tesla Roadster, an all-electric sports car. It could go from 0 to 60 miles per hour in under 4 seconds, and it had a range of about 220 miles. Arnold Schwarzenegger, the governor of California, applauded the company's efforts and encouraged Tesla to continue making these cars in his state.

Scientists and car manufacturers agree that as the public sees more electric and hybrid cars on the road, they will become more interested in purchasing one themselves. It will be like it was a hundred years ago when people moved away from electric and steam cars to gasoline-powered cars. Now people will be purchasing electric and hybrid cars, because these cars are more environmentally friendly.

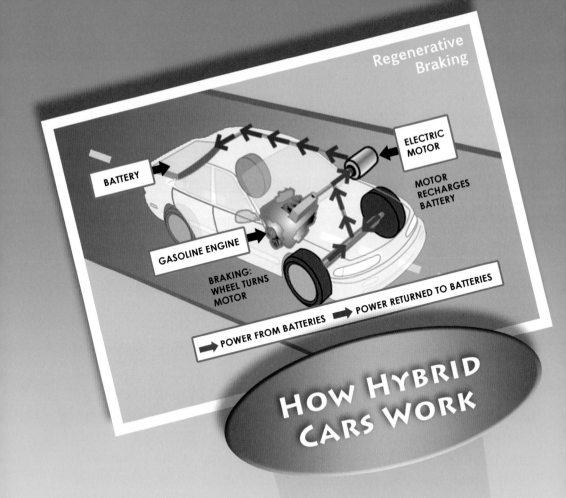

BATTERY

ELECTRIC MOTOR

MOTOR RECHARGES BATTERY

GASOLINE ENGINE

BRAKING: WHEEL TURNS MOTOR

POWER FROM BATTERIES ➡ **POWER RETURNED TO BATTERIES**

How Hybrid Cars Work

A gasoline-electric hybrid car uses a gasoline engine and an electric motor. A typical gasoline car has a fuel tank that supplies gasoline to the engine. The engine turns the **transmission**. A transmission is a set of gears that transfer power from an engine to the axle, which turns the wheels. A traditional electric car has a set of batteries that run the motor. The motor turns the axle.

The hybrid car's gasoline engine is smaller than a traditional car's, and it has advanced technologies to reduce pollution. The electric motor on a hybrid car also has special technology that lets the motor be used as a **generator**. A generator transforms mechanical energy into electrical energy. The electric motor on a hybrid car acts as a generator when the brakes are applied. As the car slows down, the motor

Hybrid
Escalade

Hybrid
Engine

charges the batteries. This process is called regenerative braking.

A hybrid car uses batteries to store energy for the electric motor. It also has a small fuel tank for the gasoline engine. The motor and engine can be used together in two different ways. In a **parallel hybrid,** both the engine and the electric motor can turn the transmission at the same time. In a **series hybrid,** the gasoline engine powers a generator, and the generator can either power the electric motor that drives transmission, or it can charge the batteries.

A hybrid car does not use the gasoline engine all the time. When a hybrid car is stopped at a traffic light, the gasoline engine turns off because it is not needed. The car uses the electric motor for power until it reaches about

40 miles per hour. If the driver wants to accelerate more quickly, the gasoline engine will kick in to aid the acceleration. When the car reaches highway speeds of 55 to 70 mph, the car runs with a combination of gasoline and electric power.

A computer in the car automatically activates the electric motor or the gasoline engine—or both—depending on how much power the car needs. The driver does not have to worry about it at all.

A plug-in hybrid car works like a gasoline hybrid. The difference is that the batteries are charged from the **electric grid** instead of from the gasoline engine. The driver simply plugs the car in when it is parked. The batteries of the car will recharge just like the batteries on a phone or camera. Because the engine does not have to charge the batteries,

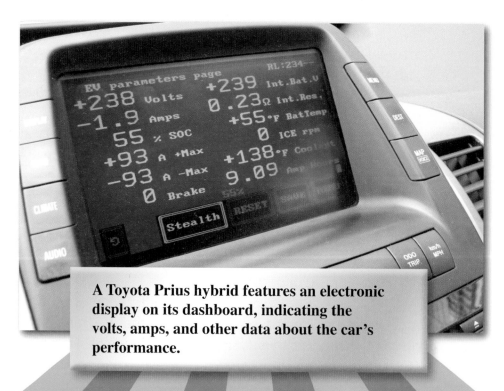

A Toyota Prius hybrid features an electronic display on its dashboard, indicating the volts, amps, and other data about the car's performance.

less gasoline is used. Less air pollution is made when the car is being driven. The trade-off is that it increases the amount of electricity that is used from the grid—and electrical production can also cause pollution.

When the car is charging, unless it is using electricity produced by solar or wind power, it is using electricity made from power plants. Electric power plants often make their electricity by burning coal or petroleum products. As the coal is burned, it pollutes the environment. However, even using electricity from power plants, the plug-in hybrid still contributes 15 percent less carbon pollution than a traditional gasoline-powered car.

Diesel-electric hybrid cars have two sources of power, just like gasoline-electric hybrid cars. Diesel-electric hybrids contain a diesel engine and an electric motor. Diesel engines burn diesel fuel instead of gasoline, and they do not use spark plugs. There is a computer system that switches between the engine and the motor.

Diesel engines have several advantages over gasoline engines. First, they burn less fuel than gasoline engines. They can also deliver much more power than gasoline engines, so they can pull heavier loads. That is why diesel engines are used to power trucks, buses, and trains.

Diesel-electric hybrid vehicles can also do big jobs. Some cities have diesel hybrid buses, and many trains are pulled by diesel-electric locomotives. The electric motors help reduce the amount of diesel that is used. Trucks and buses can still pull heavy loads but make less pollution.

A hydrogen fuel car runs a little differently than an electric or hybrid car. Instead of batteries, the hydrogen car uses hydrogen fuel cells. Hydrogen is a chemical found in nature. There is a lot of hydrogen on Earth. It is one of the most plentiful elements in the world.

When hydrogen combines with oxygen, it makes water. In science, water is called H_2O. Each **molecule** of water has two **atoms** of hydrogen (H) combined with one atom of oxygen (O). A fuel cell combines hydrogen and oxygen to make water—a process that produces electricity. The electricity that is made can be used to power a car.

Like a hybrid gasoline car, the hydrogen car is equipped with a computer. The computer regulates the flow of hydrogen across the fuel cell. The computer helps tell the car when to switch motors. It helps save fuel. And instead of putting out toxic gases, the hydrogen car's waste products are water

DID YOU KNOW...

In Europe in 2009, a gallon of gasoline cost nearly ten dollars—more than four times as expensive as gasoline in the United States. Drivers in Europe love hybrid cars because they save money. They are also interested in bio-diesel cars. European scientists are working on ways to use straw and wood to fuel cars.

The Morgan hydrogen LIFECar prototype

In a hydrogen-powered car, hydrogen is pumped into a fuel cell from a storage tank. The tank must be kept very cold so that the hydrogen is in liquid form. (Warm hydrogen is a gas, which takes up more space than the liquid.) Oxygen is taken into the car from the air. As the oxygen and hydrogen move across a proton-exchange membrane (PEM), the atoms combine to make water.

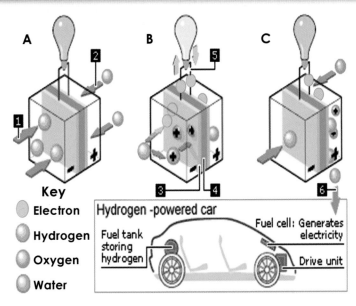

A **B** **C**

Key

⚪ **Electron**

🟤 **Hydrogen**

🟡 **Oxygen**

⚪ **Water**

Hydrogen -powered car

Fuel tank storing hydrogen

Fuel cell: Generates electricity

Drive unit

1 Hydrogen: Constantly pumped in at negative terminal
2 Oxygen: Pumped in at opposite positive terminal
3 Catalyst: Helps electrons break free from hydrogen atoms
4 Membrane: Allows hydrogen ions through but blocks electrons
5 Circuit: Electrons flow through circuit to positive terminal
6 Electrons and hydrogen ions combine with oxygen, forming water

The PEM is placed between a positively charged electrode called a cathode, and a negatively charged electrode, called an anode. When hydrogen gas is pumped into the fuel cell, it first passes through the anode. This causes a chemical reaction that breaks the hydrogen atom into protons and electrons. Both the electrons and protons are drawn to the cathode on the other side of the fuel cell. Only the protons can pass through the PEM. The electrons are forced to go around the membrane and into a circuit. The electrons in the circuit generate the electricity that runs the car.

The protons pass through the PEM, where they join with oxygen atoms. They combine to produce H_2O, or water.

Toyota's Hybrid-X is a gasoline-electric hybrid that promises to be more fuel-efficient while creating less pollution than the Prius.

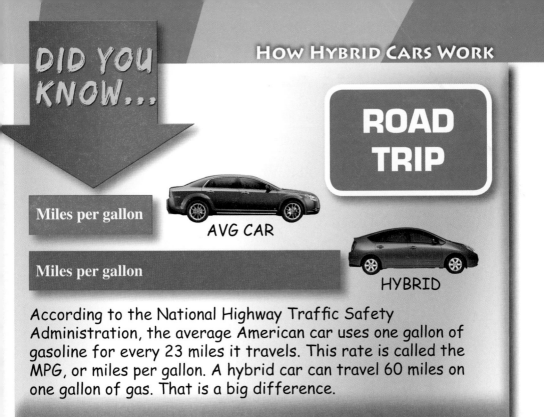

DID YOU KNOW...

ROAD TRIP

Miles per gallon

AVG CAR

Miles per gallon

HYBRID

According to the National Highway Traffic Safety Administration, the average American car uses one gallon of gasoline for every 23 miles it travels. This rate is called the MPG, or miles per gallon. A hybrid car can travel 60 miles on one gallon of gas. That is a big difference.

and a small amount of nitrogen oxide. It is a very clean car.

For decades, students and inventors have been working on solar-powered cars, which use sunshine for fuel. These cars use **photovoltaic** cells to power the electric motor. These cells are made from silicon. The silicon reacts with sunlight and produces an electric charge. Electricity from the photovoltaic cells is used to power the motor or to charge the batteries.

In the future, it may be possible for electric cars to provide energy to their owners. Scientists are experimenting with ways to take the energy stored in electric car batteries and return it to the electric grid. Electric companies would pay car owners for the electricity they send. Meanwhile, drivers would reduce the pollution caused by electric plants.

Solar hybrid Quaranta

You may think driving a hybrid car sounds really great, but if you are too young to drive, how can you help?

One thing you can do is talk to your family about what type of car they want to drive. You can explain to them that there are many different types of cars on the market right now. Almost every major car manufacturer sells some type of hybrid or electric vehicle. Many car dealers even have hybrid cars on their lots. Your family can test-drive one to see how it works.

The price of a hybrid car is sometimes higher than the price of a gasoline-powered car. But the prices of hybrids are dropping. In 2009, there were eight car manufacturers offering hybrid cars for $25,000 or less. The Toyota Prius cost about $24,000. A gasoline-powered Toyota Camry cost about

1973 GM Urban Electric Car

Electric Suburu, 2008

$21,000. People who buy hybrid cars may be able to get a tax credit from the U.S. government, and some individual states like California also offer tax cuts to people who buy hybrid cars. These tax benefits will help offset the higher price of hybrid cars.

You can also help the environment by writing letters to lawmakers. Let them know you will support laws that will make hybrid cars more affordable. Ask the lawmakers to give tax cuts for people who buy clean-air cars. And tell them how important it is for the planet to have clean air, soil, and water. You won't be alone in your requests. Governor Arnold Schwarzenegger wrote to President Barack Obama and asked him to consider ways to allow California to continue its efforts to reduce air pollution there.

You can also talk to your friends and teachers or club leaders. Explain how much pollution is caused by cars. Tell them that according to the Environmental Protection Agency, cars are the largest producers of pollution in the world. By changing the cars they drive, people can help save the environment.

Remember that some of the new types of cars are very expensive. Even if your family can afford a hybrid car, they may not be ready to replace the car they have. Most families use their cars for several years before they purchase a different one.

Just because your family doesn't own a hybrid car doesn't mean you can't reduce your carbon footprint. Helping your

You can help your family reduce the pollution their car causes by helping them with regular oil changes and car maintenance.

family keep the car in good running order is important. This includes having the car's engine tuned by a mechanic to keep the engine running as cleanly as possible. A clean-running engine causes less pollution.

Remind your family to get the oil changed on a regular basis. When you get the oil changed, make sure to recycle the oil. If you have your oil changed at a car repair shop, the repairman will recycle the oil for you. If a family member changes the oil, be sure he or she takes it to a special recycling station. Oil recycling stations are listed in the phone book and on the Internet.

Have an adult check the air pressure in the tires. Too little air can make a car use more gas than it should. Look in your owner's manual to find out what the air pressure in your tires should be.

Check your car to be sure it is wind efficient. Things like luggage racks and bicycle racks can make your car use more gasoline. Take off all racks when they are not being used. You should also check that your gasoline cap has a tight seal. Gasoline evaporates easily, so a tight gas cap can save fuel and reduce pollution. And don't forget to clean out the trunk. Carrying extra weight in the car burns more gasoline. Don't carry around heavy loads when you don't have to.

You can also help the environment by not using the car at all. Try riding your bicycle to do errands. Bicycles do not pollute the air, and you get exercise. You could also walk to the store. Just be sure to get permission before you go.

Another way to save fuel and help reduce pollution is to ride public transportation, such as the bus. When people ride the bus, there are fewer cars on the road. If you don't have a bus system in town, you can carpool. Get your friends together and ride in the same car when you have to go to ballgames or school events. By sharing a ride, you will save

An electric Smart car plugged in and recharging. This scene could become more common every day.

DID YOU KNOW...

Louis Palmer proved that you can go anywhere there are roads in an electric car. He drove around the world in a three-wheeled solar electric car. The Swiss school teacher drove through 38 countries and over 32,000 miles without using any gasoline. He also planned to drive around the world in 80 days, using six different alternative-fuel vehicles.

gasoline. For long trips, consider taking a train. When many people travel on a train, it saves energy.

You can make posters that tell about car pollution and how to decrease it. Ask if you can hang your posters in your school or in businesses in your town. Your poster will remind people to do what they can to reduce pollution.

Be creative! Maybe your posters can show how riding bikes and walking will help stop pollution. Then get your friends together with their bicycles, scooters, and skateboards and hold a pollution-free vehicle parade.

Ask your principal or teacher if you can have an environment day at school. You could have students give reports on hybrid and electric cars and how they help the planet. Invite parents and community members. Anyone can learn from you and your friends.

Use your imagination. You can come up with all sorts of fun ways to teach people about hybrid and electric cars. It is important to share what you have learned. Saving the environment will take everybody's help. And just like Cameron Diaz, Brad Pitt, and Al Gore, you can work with others to make the earth a greener place to live.

TRY THIS!

Air Pollution Experiment

You will need:

3 sheets of white paper
   or cardboard
petroleum jelly
masking tape
a sunny day
magnifying glass

It is best to do this experiment when the weather will be sunny for several days.

Cover two sheets of paper on one side with the petroleum jelly. Tape the two sheets of paper to the outside of your window. Make sure the petroleum side faces out. Take the plain sheet of paper inside the house.

At the end of the day, take one of the sheets off the window. Take it inside and compare it to the sheet of paper you left inside the house. Which one is cleaner? Save both sheets of paper.

Wait three days and bring in the last sheet of paper. Compare it to the other two pieces of paper. Which one is cleanest? Which one is dirtiest? Use a magnifying glass to see more details.

The petroleum jelly will collect the pollution that is in the air outside. You can see just how dirty the air in your neighborhood is.

Historical Timeline

1769 Nicolas-Joseph Cugnot invents the first self-propelled road vehicle. It runs on steam.

1807 Isaac de Rivas invents a hydrogen-powered vehicle.

c.1839 Robert Anderson of Aberdeen, Scotland, builds the first electric vehicle.

1863 Jean Lenoir drives fifty miles in a petroleum-powered automobile.

1867 The first motorcycle is invented.

1870 Sir David Salomon develops a car with an electric motor and very heavy storage batteries. The weight keeps the car from traveling very fast or very far.

1885 Karl Benz builds the first automobile to be powered by an internal combustion gasoline engine. Gottlieb Daimler attaches an internal combustion engine to a stagecoach to make the first four-wheeled automobile.

1886 An electric-powered taxicab that uses a battery with 28 cells and a small electric motor is used in England.

1893 Rudolf Diesel lays the groundwork for an internal combustion engine that can run on vegetable oil.

1897 The London Electric Cab Company begins regular service using electric cars designed by Walter Bersey. They have a 3-horsepower motor and can drive 50 miles between charges.

1898 At twenty-three years old, Ferdinand Porsche builds his first car. It is called the Lohner Electric Chaise.

1901 Porsche's second car is the Mixte Hybrid, which uses both a gasoline engine and an electric motor. On battery alone, the car could travel nearly 40 miles.

1900 American car companies make 1,681 steam, 1,575 electric, and 936 gasoline cars. The first National Automobile Show is held in New York City. Visitors prefer electric and steam cars over the gasoline models.

1904 The Electric Vehicle Company builds 2,000 taxicabs, trucks, and buses. About 57 smaller auto plants, make about 4,000 cars.

1913 With the invention of the electric starter, the gasoline car becomes the people's favorite type of vehicle. Henry Ford sells 182,809 gasoline cars; only 6,000 electric cars are purchased.

1914 Henry Ford revolutionizes the auto industry by improving the assembly line for manufacturing.

Historical Timeline

1920–65 The gasoline engine rules the world. Only scientists and inventors work with electric cars and alternative fuel cars.

1966 The U.S. Congress recommends building cars with electric motors as a way to reduce air pollution.

1970s The price of gasoline skyrockets, and people begin looking at more fuel-efficient cars or cars that will run on alternative fuels.

1972 The Electric Datsun is made, but is not for mass-production.

1976 The U.S. Congress passes a law that will help car manufacturers develop electric and hybrid vehicles.

1978 The Energy Tax Act establishes the Gas Guzzler Tax, which is applied to new cars whose fuel economy is below a certain level.

1980 Briggs and Stratton invents a hybrid car powered by a gasoline engine and an electric motor. It has six wheels: two in the front and four in the back.

1989 Audi builds its first experimental electric car.

1992 The Toyota Motor Company announces the Earth Charter. Its goal is to develop cars with the lowest pollution in the world.

1997 The Toyota Prius is introduced in Japan. It is a gasoline-electric hybrid car. In the first year, 18,000 of these cars are sold.

1997–99 American car manufacturers introduce several all-electric cars in California. They do not sell well, and car makers stop producing them.

1999 Honda introduces the hybrid Insight to the United States.

2000 Toyota brings the hybrid Prius to the United States.

2002 Honda introduces the Honda Civic Hybrid to the United States.

2006 Tesla Motors introduces its all-electric Roadster.

2007 Many other car manufacturers begin offering hybrid cars, including Lexus, Ford, Nissan, Chevrolet, and Mazda Dodge.

2008 Hybrid and alternative-fuel cars become more and more popular with the public. Demand for pollution-free cars keeps increasing.

2009 The Chevrolet Volt is honored with Green Car Journal's 2009 Green Car Vision Award™ at the Washington Auto Show.

Further Reading

Hammond, Richard. *Car Science.* New York: DK Children's Books, 2008.

Knight, M.J. *Why Should I Walk More Often?* North Mankato, MN: Smart Apple Media, 2008.

Povey, Karen D. *Hybrid Cars.* Chicago: Kid Haven Press, 2006.

Walker, Niki. *Hydrogen: Running On Water.* New York: Crabtree Publishing, 2007.

Wheeler, Jill C. *Alternative Cars.* Edina, MA: Checkerboard Books, 2007.

Works Consulted

Bauers, Sandy. "Electric Car Returns Energy to the Grid." *Philadelphia Inquirer,* February 6, 2009. http://www.philly.com/inquirer/magazine/20090202_Electric_car_returns_energy_to_the_grid.html

Begley, Ed, Jr. *Living Like Ed.* New York: Clarkson Potter Publishers, 2008.

Boschert, Sherry. *Plug-in Hybrids: The Cars That Will Recharge America.* Gabriola Island, British Columbia: New Society Publishers, 2007.

della Cava, Marco R. "Celebs Do Their Part at Home, on Road." *USA TODAY,* August 30, 2004. http://www.usatoday.com/life/people/2004-08-30-eco-celebs-side_x.htm

———. "Danny Seo, Rolling in Green." USA TODAY, August 30, 2004. http://www.usatoday.com/life/people/2004-08-30-danny-seo_x.htm

"Eco-Celebrity Brad Pitt." Treehugger.com, December 8, 2004. http://www.treehugger.com/files/2004/12/ecoceleb_brad_p.php

Fuhs, Allen. *Hybrid Vehicles and the Future of Personal Transportation.* Boca Raton, FL: CRC Press, 2008.

FuturePundit. "Plug-In Hybrid Car Pollution Benefits Seen as Small." September 24, 2006. http://www.futurepundit.com/archives/003744.html

"Gore Calls for Electric Vehicle Future." HybridCars.com, July 18, 2008. http://www.hybridcars.com/oil-dependence/gore-calls-electric-vehicle-future-0718.html

Haredeski, Michael Frank. *Alternative Fuels: The Future of Hydrogen.* Lilburn, GA: Fairmon Press, 2006.

"Honda Makes First Hydrogen Cars." BBC, June 16, 2008. http://news.bbc.co.uk/2/hi/business/7456141.stm

Works Consulted

Hybrid Vehicle History: More than a Century of Evolution and Refinement.
http://www.hybrid-vehicle.org/hybrid-vehicle-history.html

Kageyama, Yuri. "AP: Toyota Secretly Developing Solar Powered Green Car." *Huffington Post,* January 1, 2009.
http://www.huffingtonpost.com/2009/01/01/ap-toyota-secretly-develo_n_154654.html

Lee, David W. *Good Car-Ma Bad Car-Ma.* Scotts Valley, CA: CreateSpace Publishing, 2008.

Motavalli, Jim. "Prius Diaz and the Hollywood Hybrids." *Electrifying Times,* July 17, 2002. http://www.electrifyingtimes.com/priusdiaz.html

Motor Trend: "New Hybrid Cars," 2009. http://www.motortrend.com/new_cars/27/hybrid_cars/index.html

Nerad, Jack R. *The Complete Idiot's Guide to Hybrid and Alternative Fuel Vehicles.* New York: Alpha Books, 2007.

Vehicle Recycling Partnership
http://www.uscar.org/guest/article_view.php?articles_id=233

Winter, Jozef. "Prius Hits 1 M in Sales, Saves 450 M Tons of Carbon." EcoGeek, May 23, 2008.
http://www.ecogeek.org/content/view/1669/69/

On the Internet

Chevron Cars: Car Fun Facts
http://www.chevroncars.com/learn/cars/car-fun-facts

Environmental Protection Agency: Environmental Kids Club
http://www.epa.gov/kids/

Fuel Economy.gov: "How Hybrids Work"
http://www.fueleconomy.gov/Feg/hybridtech.shtml

Global Green USA
http://www.globalgreen.org/

Kids 4 Clean Air: Information Sheets
http://www.clean-air-kids.org.uk/information.html

Science News for Kids: Revving Up Green Machines
http://www.sciencenewsforkids.org/articles/20050608/Feature1.asp

Wisconsin Department of Natural Resources: Environmental Education for Kids
http://www.dnr.state.wi.us/eek/

Glossary

accelerating (ak-SEH-luh-ray-ting)—Picking up speed.

atom (AA-tum)—One of the building blocks of matter.

bio-diesel (BY-oh-dee-sul)—Fuel for engines made from the oils of plants such as corn and soybeans.

carbon footprint—The amount of pollution caused by one person, household, or company.

conservation (kon-ser-VAY-shun)— Planned management and protection of natural resources.

electric grid—The system that transfers electricity generated in power companies to homes, businesses, and other consumers.

fossil fuels (FAH-sul fyoolz)—Energy sources drilled or mined from the earth, such as petroleum oil and coal.

generator (JEH-nuh-ray-tur)—A machine that changes mechanical energy (motion) into electricity.

global warming (GLOH-bul WAR-ming)—An increase in the world's temperatures caused by the greenhouse effect.

green—Living in a way that respects our natural resources and protects people and other things that live on the planet, now and in the future.

hybrid (HY-brid) **car**—A vehicle that uses two or more power sources.

hydrogen (HY-droh-jen)—The lightest element and the most abundant in the universe.

molecule (MAH-lih-kyool)— The smallest group of atoms that still make up a substance. For example, a group of two hydrogen atoms and one oxygen atom makes up one molecule of water.

muffler (MUF-ler)—A cylindrical part on an exhaust pipe that reduces the amount of noise emitted by the engine.

nonrenewable (non-ree-NOO-uh-bul)—Unable to be made again.

ozone (OH-zohn)—A gas that protects the earth from harmful rays of the sun, but too much of it can destroy the atmosphere.

Glossary

petroleum (peh-TROH-lee-um)—An oily substance found under the surface of the earth that can be refined to make gasoline, diesel fuel, and other fuels.

photovoltaic (foh-toh-vol-TAY-ik)—Making or using electricity produced from sunlight.

plug-in hybrid—A vehicle that uses the two power sources of gasoline and electricity but also has a way to plug in to an electrical outlet to charge batteries.

pollution (puh-LOO-shun)—Something unclean, such as chemicals and poisonous substances introduced into the environment.

refined (ree-FIND)—Made pure by an industrial process.

regenerative (ree-JEH-nuh-rih-tiv) **braking**—In electric vehicles, the process of charging the battery by braking, which makes the generator send electricity to the battery instead of to the axle.

renewable resource (ree-NOO-uh-bul REE-sors)—A supply of energy that can be used over and over again because more can be produced.

smog—A mixture of fog, smoke, and other air pollutants such as exhaust fumes.

transmission (trans-MIH-shun)—A set of gears that transfer power from an engine to the axle, which turns the wheels.

2009 Honda Insight Hybrid

Index

Stephanie Bearce grew up on a farm in Kansas where the skies were blue and she never saw the fog of pollution. Then she moved to a large city where there were lots of cars and very little public transportation. On summer days the skies were often hazy and gray from smog.

Bearce became interested in learning how to help clean the environment. She worked as a teacher and education coordinator at Missouri Botanical Garden, where scientists research how plants and humans can help the earth. She learned about alternative fuel sources for homes and cars and worked to teach adults and children. As a science teacher, she worked with students to research science fair projects that show the benefits of alternative fuels.

In the future Bearce hopes that hybrid and electric cars will become a normal form of transportation—and that smog will be a distant memory for all people.